To Joan:
Thank you for the
support & friendship.
Best wishes + stay safe.
Chief Fitt (2009)

She Bear

Empowerment & Safety for Women

BY

**PAT McKINLEY
CHIEF of POLICE**

TESORO
publishing

**TESORO PUBLISHING
FULLERTON, CA 2008**

She Bear
Tesoro Publishing
PO Box 528
Fullerton, CA 92836
www.tesoropublishing.com

ISBN 978-0-9797419-5-1

Copyright 2009 by Tesoro Publishing

First Edition

All rights reserved. No part of this book may be reproduced or utilized in any way for or by any means electronic or mechanical, including photocopying, recording or by information storage or revival system without permission in writing from the Publisher.

Some names used in this book have been changed to protect the individuals involved.

Disclaimer: The audience of this book is aimed at teenagers and adults. The advice in this book does not apply to victims of childhood abuse in which the child has no way of using the techniques heretofore mentioned in the book. If you suspect child abuse, please call 1-800 HELP A CHILD available 24 hours a day, 7 days a week.

Library of Congress Control Number: Pending

Printed in the United States of America

This book has been written and published strictly for informational purposes, and in no way should be used as a substitute for actual instruction with qualified professionals for self defense. The author and publisher are providing you with information in this work so that you can have the knowledge and can choose, at your own risk, to act on that knowledge. The author and publisher also urge all readers to be aware of their health status and to consult health care professionals before beginning any health program.

Author:Pat McKinley
Editors:Emily Roberts, Staci Homrig
Cover and Book Design:Helen Butler at Helen Butler Graphics

DEDICATION

Dedicated to Samantha (Sam) Hendershot
"A Ferocious She Bear"

ACKNOWLEDGEMENTS

I want to extend my gratitude to the following individuals for their assistance in editing and giving advice to make the book that much better: Emily Roberts and Staci Homrig, Editors, Kathleen Hodge, EdD, Dr. Jo Ann Brannock, Yolanda Aguirre, Narina Gonneville and Monica Roberts.

Thanks to Helen Butler for her part in shaping the look of the book. Thanks you also to Anthony Bach for his beautiful cover art.

To all the She Bears and their stories that are included in this book, I want to extend my gratitude. I want to thank you not only for your part in this book, but for the courage and strength you have shown in the most difficult of circumstances.

I want to thank every She Bear who has attended one of my lectures for their insight and support.

Most importantly, I want to thank my wife for her continued support and encouragement, without which I never would have been able to write this book.

TABLE OF CONTENTS

ABOUT THE AUTHOR 1
INTRODUCTION 3
1   **WHAT IS A SHE BEAR?** 7
2   **OVERCOMING FEAR** 11
3   **DISBELIEF, DISORIENTATION AND OVERWHELMING FEAR** 17
4   **STEP 1: LISTEN TO YOUR INNER SENSE OF DANGER** 21
5   **STEP 2: CHANGE YOUR MINDSET** 25
6   **SMARTS WINNING OVER STRENGTH** 31
7   **SITUATIONS TO AVOID** 37
8   **SIMPLE SAFETY TECHNIQUES** 43
9   **HOME SAFETY** 49
10 **CAR SAFETY** 55
11 **DATE RAPE** 63
12 **STALKING** 67
13 **SURVIVING A HOSTAGE CRISIS** 71
14 **SURVIVING WITH DIGNITY** 75
15 **A SURVIVOR OF AN ATTEMPTED ABDUCTION** 79
16 **A SURVIVOR OF AN ATTEMPTED KIDNAPPING** 89
17 **NEVER QUIT FIGHTING** 95
QUICK SUMMARY 99
INDEX 101

ABOUT THE AUTHOR

Chief Pat McKinley is a 44-year veteran of law enforcement. After serving four years in the United States Air Force, he attended the police academy in Los Angeles. He then went on to work for the L.A. Police Department for 29 years. He started as a patrol officer, working a beat in South Central L.A. and skid row, and then worked his way up the ranks to captain in 15 years. He retired from the LAPD in 1993, and relocated to Fullerton, California, where he assumed the job of chief of police at the Fullerton Police Department.

Among his achievements as a police officer, McKinley considers his work with the Los Angeles Police Department's (LAPD) Special Weapons and Tactics unit (SWAT) the most fulfilling. In 1968 he and 75 other officers volunteered to be part of an elite force within the LAPD that was trained to use military-style tactics and equipment during high-pressure incidents in which suspects had barricaded themselves inside a home or building. The objective of the SWAT unit was to extract suspects and bring them to justice as safely and efficiently as possible. During his 25 years of working with the SWAT team, McKinley was involved in more than 100 incidents involving barricaded suspects – from kidnappings to bank robberies to stalkings that turned into hostage situations.

He has a Master's Degree in Business Administration from the University of Southern California, and has trained at the FBI National Academy in Quantico, Virginia. He also attended Dignitary Protection School offered by the United States

Secret Service in Washington, D.C., to learn the skills and tactics necessary for keeping high-profile protectees safe when they are in public settings. For the past 20 years, he has been on faculty at Fullerton College and Rio Hondo College in Southern California where he teaches police officer safety, weaponless defense and tactical awareness. He also has taught police officer training courses through the U.S. State Department and Harper & Row's Criminal Justice Seminars.

His extensive training and experience with barricaded suspects have taught him volumes about the criminal mind. He learned that most criminals are weak-willed and skittish. The slightest resistance from a potential victim will send him or her looking for someone else to victimize. In an effort to understand this phenomenon, McKinley talked to victims and other officers who have debriefed victims over the years. McKinley also gained insight into what causes a person to be a victim in the first place. In *She Bear*, McKinley shares this knowledge with female readers who want to overcome becoming a victim, along with her fears and stereotypical politeness to be a fierce protective fighter.

INTRODUCTION

In 1980, while I was working as a captain in the 77th Street Division of the Los Angeles Police Department, a good friend – who happened to be the Alhambra police chief – called to tell me about a horrible incident that had happened. The wife of one of the officers under my command had been brutally beaten and raped, her injuries so severe that she was in the hospital. My friend asked me to notify the officer and accompany him to the hospital. The officer was on duty in the field in a patrol car so I asked dispatch to have the officer report to my office right away.

When the patrol officer arrived in my office, I knew immediately we had a long night ahead of us. The unsuspecting officer had no idea why he had been summoned. He stood in my office looking every bit the model police officer. His uniform was impeccable. He was in excellent physical condition. This perfection was in stark contrast to the bewildered expression on his face. He appeared worried that he might be chastised for something, and his mind was running in over-drive trying to determine what the infraction might be and what defense he might need to take. I knew that once I opened my mouth, he would have preferred me to yell at him rather than hear the devastating message I had to deliver.

I was direct and to the point. I said: "Your wife has been raped. She is not dead. She is in the hospital. You and I will go there now." I saw that officer's knees start to buckle and he nearly fell to the floor. Remember – this is an experienced, tough police officer who was working a very active division. He had seen more human conflict in a year than the average person would see in a lifetime. His toughness and self-assuredness evaporated as he asked me questions I could not answer.

When we arrived at the hospital, the officer's wife was lying on a hospital gurney in the emergency room. Her face was swollen; both eyes were black. It was clear she had suffered a merciless beating. At first I stayed several feet away, not wanting to interfere in this moment of truth as the officer's harsh work life collided with his private family life. The medical staff was doing a professional job caring for her physical and medical needs, but nobody approached the young woman to talk to her and console her. The police officer stood immobile, a look of shocked disbelief on his face. The chaos of the emergency room buzzed all around us, but the officer stood stalk still.

After what seemed like an eternity, I stepped forward and took her hand. I kissed her on the forehead and said, "Honey, you're safe now. No one will hurt you again." This was the first time I had ever seen the young police officer's wife. We had never spoken before. But I will never forget how she squeezed my hand and started to cry. As the clock ticked on, I continued to hold her hand and gaze down at her bruised and battered body. I thought about how incredibly unfair and cruel life could be. Such a sweet, young woman should not have had to suffer as she did, and I vowed, in that moment, to do something about it. I vowed to share my training, experience and knowledge with other women so that they could learn to use their God-given skills to avoid danger and fight back.

I held true to my vision and commitment. Since that night in the emergency room, I have lectured to more than a thousand women on my training program titled "She Bear." Every lecture is an opportunity for me to personally reach out to women and reassure them that they have the power to overcome their Disbelief, Disorientation, and Overwhelming Fear – that they have the power to be a "She Bear." All of my lectures follow the same rule – women only. No man has ever heard the lecture and for good reason. When I talk to women about changing their mindset and employing some of the simple techniques I discuss later in this book, I want them to feel safe, comfortable and unencumbered by old patterns and stereotypes. I know that the things I discuss in this book and in my lectures evoke strong emotions, both in me and in members of the audience. I want to ensure that the lines of communication stay open and participants are comfortable in the environment with no embarrassment.

Out of the tragedy of the police officer's wife grew a lifelong commitment to women's safety. When I retire from the Fullerton Police Department in 2009, I plan to continue sharing my insights with women across the country. I hope that this book will empower readers to find the strong, confident powerhouse that lies within every woman. Out of the tragedy of the police officer's wife came the inspiration for the book you are holding in your hand. After reading the tactics and truths in the pages to follow, you will be 80% safer and able to call yourself a "She Bear."

She Bear

Chapter 1

What is a She Bear?

I was raised as a country boy. I grew up on farms in South Dakota and Minnesota in the 1940s and 50s, and one of the lessons I learned was that it's better to be a grizzly bear than a frog.

When I was about 8 or 9 years old, I came upon a hand-dug well that was about ten feet deep. At the bottom of the well, there was a small pool of water and an old wooden ladder that stretched all the way to the surface above. I laid on my stomach in the grass and peered down the rungs of the ladder to the darkness below. On the bottom rung of the ladder there was a frog looking up at me. After my eyes adjusted to the darkness, I realized he wasn't staring at me; he was staring at a garter snake that was slowly slithering down the ladder.

That frog mesmerized me. It was clear that he saw the snake. All he had to do to live was jump out of the hole. I kept thinking, "OK, Mr Frog, anytime now. I know you're going to jump because you must realize that snake is not your friend." But that snake just kept sliding down the ladder and the frog just sat frozen, watching him. Well, perhaps you can guess what happened. In short order, the snake reached the bottom rung, opened his unhinged jaw and devoured the frog. The frog never moved an inch.

After 44 years in law enforcement, I now know why that frog fell prey to a slower, less skillful predator. He suffered from a paralysis based in Disbelief, Disorientation and Overwhelming Fear.

When you are confronted with a frightening situation that takes you completely out of your experience base, you go through three stages. First, you experience Disbelief. You tell yourself, "Whatever is happening cannot possibly be happening to me." Second, you become Disoriented. You feel a sensation of vertigo or an out-of-body experience in which it appears that the situation is happening to someone else. Third, you experience Overwhelming Fear – the kind of fear that locks your feet into one spot and closes your throat so you can't scream.

Disbelief, Disorientation and Overwhelming Fear are what caused that frog to sit frozen on the ladder while his enemy approached. This is the same phenomenon that can cause many strong, capable women to fall prey to criminals. In this book I will help you learn to use the tools you already possess to avoid behaving like the frog.

The fiercest animal in the forest is the female grizzly bear. *Ursus horribilis* is the most aggressive of all the bears and she has no predators. A full-grown male grizzly bear can weigh as much as 1,150 pounds, outweighing the female by about 400 pounds. In addition to nuts and berries, the male grizzly bear preys on moose, mountain goats, sheep and even bear cubs that dare to get in his way of mating with a female grizzly bear.

Never the less, a female grizzly bear protecting her cubs is the force to be reckoned with in the wild. She will swat at a male grizzly with no reservations. She will claw, bite, kick and scratch, and nine times out of 10 she will make a male grizzly realize it's not worth the effort. The male grizzly bear will turn tail and walk away.

The reason a female grizzly can prevail over a male grizzly, who is stronger and weighs one-third more than she does, is because she is fighting for something and he is not. When you fight for something, you fight smart and you fight hard. You look for opportunities to defeat your opponent, and you use every tool in your arsenal. The criminals who are out there waiting to take advantage of you are not tough. They don't take care of themselves. They don't train physically. They don't eat the proper foods. They smoke. They drink. They do drugs. They abuse and debilitate their bodies. They are not mentally or physically strong people. They have little will. And if they meet resistance, they crumble. I realize this is inconsistent with perceptions of the hard, tough street criminals. This is why it's important to address the myth that the men who sexually assault women have the mental and physical upper hand.

This book will demonstrate how every woman is born with the tools to make these criminals turn tail and walk away. It is about setting aside society's preconceived notions that women must be nice or polite in all situations. It is about learning to trust your Inner Sense of Danger. It is about overcoming the Disbelief, Disorientation and Overwhelming Fear that grips you when you are confronted with a frightening situation. It is about finding the "She Bear" that is inside each and every woman.

Chapter 2

Overcoming Fear

In December 1966 cousins Myron Lance and Walter Kelbach went on a killing spree in Utah. The night of December 17, 1966, the two men were under the influence of drugs and alcohol and drove to an all-night gas station in Salt Lake City where 18-year-old Stephen Shea was working alone. They robbed Shea of $147 at gunpoint, forced him into the back seat of their station wagon and drove him into the Utah desert. They forced Shea to strip and then raped him. After the assault, they flipped a coin to decide which one of them would kill him. Kelbach won; he stabbed Shea five times in the chest and threw his body into a roadside ditch. The next night the two went to another all-night gas station where Michael Holtz was working alone. They robbed Holtz, kidnapped and raped him, and killed him in the same manner.

A few days later, Lance and Kelbach hopped into the backseat of a taxi with the intention of robbing the driver. As the taxi arrived at the requested destination, Lance immediately pulled out a gun and demanded that the driver give him all his money, which turned out to be $9. Angry, Lance shot the driver through the head. The two then moved on to Lolly's Tavern, near the Salt Lake City Airport. In the bar they brandished their guns and shouted to the dumbfounded patrons, "This is a stickup." To show they were serious, Lance and Kelbach began shooting patrons at random. Three patrons were shot and killed. Following an intensive search and pursuit, the duo was arrested, convicted and sentenced to death. They escaped execution when the United States Supreme Court wrestled with the constitutionality of capital punishment, and were sentenced to life in prison.

Veteran journalist Carl Stern interviewed Lance and Kelbach for NBC while they were in the Utah State Prison. I remember watching the broadcast with fascination. Lance and Kelbach were brutally honest in the interview – the kind of honesty associated with being a sociopath: unaware of the evil in their actions. They showed no remorse, and they often laughed and joked about the killings. Their lack of remorse, however, was not the most shocking part of the interview. I was struck most by their description of the lack of resistance by their victims.

Lance and Kelbach described the killings in detail. Stern then asked the men whether any of their victims resisted. The two looked at each other and said, "No, no." Then one of the killers said, "I remember one time we were flipping a coin and the kid said, 'what are you flipping a coin for?' And I said, 'we're trying to decide who is going to kill you.'" Then the other killer told Stern, "As I was staring at the kid, he said, 'Oh my God, I've got a wife.'"

The victim didn't resist. He didn't run. He didn't even try to escape. He knew that death was coming, but he attempted nothing to stop it. The young man was like the frog at the bottom of the well. He saw the snakes bearing down on him, but he was frozen in fear. This fear is the typical response to aggressive physical threat – no resistance. Changing this reaction is critical to survival.

This idea of paralyzing fear in the face of death is not unique to young gas station attendants. I am sure most readers are familiar with a very successful author by the name of Joseph Wambaugh. Wambaugh is a former police officer for the LAPD. He has written several fictional novels and even created and consulted for the television series "Police Story." Despite Wambaugh's success with fiction, it is one of his non-fiction books that stays with me to this day. In 1987 Joe published a book called *Lines and Shadows* about the relationship of police officers and illegal immigrants crossing the California/Mexico border in San Diego.

In the 1970s illegal immigrants streamed across the California/Mexico border – sometimes as a many as 10,000 a week. As the sun set in the west, the travelers, called *pollos*, set off for the few square miles of no-man's land that separates Tijuana, Mexico, from San Diego,

California. Prior to crossing into America, the pollos had saved their money for years and had gathered all of their belongings for their journey to a new life. But, as the travelers prepared to cross, bandit gangs huddled in the shadows on the California side, waiting to rob, rape and murder them.

Lines and Shadows is about a group of San Diego police officers tasked with playing decoy for the bandit gangs so they could arrest them and prevent the victimization of immigrants walking onto California soil. After months of crawling around the canyons, two veteran police officers began to compare notes about their fears. Both had served in the U.S. Military and seen action in Vietnam, but both considered the decoy operation far more frightening. They weren't alone in their opinion. Other officers who did not serve in Vietnam described similar feelings about the operation. After talking to these officers, Wambaugh captured their fear in the passages of *Lines and Shadows*.

I read *Lines and Shadows* after I had been a police officer for decades, dealing with danger on a daily basis. But, one line – "the terror and archetypal horror of being murdered" – made the hairs on the back of my neck stand on end. That young gas station attendant who watched the coin toss to decide whether he was stabbed to death by Lance or Kelbach, and that frog in the well must have had that terrible thought. Reading that line helped me understand how a person can freeze in the face of death. The paralysis that prevents someone from resisting is a result of three things: Disbelief, Disorientation and Overwhelming Fear.

She Bear

Chapter 3

Disbelief, Disorientation and Overwhelming Fear

Disbelief

Robbery and rape victims often report thinking, "This cannot possibly be happening." And they mistakenly think that everything will be okay since it must all just be a dream or hallucination.

Years ago, I participated in sport parachuting through an organization called the Parachute Club of America. In addition to training people to parachute safely, the club monitored sport parachuting fatalities and tried to determine the cause. If you have ever parachuted, you know that every parachutist is always equipped with a main chute and an emergency chute. If the main chute ever fails, you are supposed to deploy the emergency chute and everything should be fine. The Parachute Club of

America found that most of the fatalities it studied occurred when main parachutes failed to open and the parachutist did not deploy the emergency chute. The parachutists failed to act.

Parachutists who have survived one of these terrifying freefalls report a sense of disbelief. They think: "This cannot be happening." The majority of victims who failed to deploy the reserve chute, in an activity dominated by men, were women.

Disorientation

In addition to disbelief, people who confront a frightening situation report a feeling of disorientation or disconnectedness. There is a feeling of vertigo – a loss of time and place.

In the past 40 years I have encountered a number of rape victims in the emergency room following the assault. They all seem to have that same look – the 500-mile stare. When I or one of my officers asks, "Are you okay," most answer the same: "Yeah, I'm fine." Well, of course they are not fine, and days later, the words start to flow – the words that describe their horrible ordeal. Inevitably, they describe a scene like those experienced by people who have suffered a near-death experience. They describe a sense of floating above their own body and watching the rape happen to someone else. It's that disorientation that keep them frozen on the concrete while their assailant brutalizes their body. Disorientation needs to be conquered.

Overwhelming Fear

The final stage in the paralysis process is a feeling of overwhelming fear – the kind that touches your heart and soul. A fear so deep that the victim shakes and cries.

A fear so powerful that it renders the victim helpless and pliable. Too often, assailants start their attack with a grab at a woman's blouse. He pulls at the fabric, rips at the zipper, snaps off the buttons. Next, he grabs at her bra and yanks it from her body. A woman's natural reaction is to retreat into modesty and cover her breasts. She usually shrieks in fear and shock and then resorts to sobs and pleas. "Please, don't hurt me," she says. Unfortunately, that is exactly the reaction sought by rapists. They want to hear the cries and pleas because they know it means the woman is too overcome with fear and emotion to fight back. It is that Overwhelming Fear that keeps her frozen in place while he takes advantage of her helplessness and takes pleasure in his dominance. This stereotypical, learned behavior for women can be substituted with empowering behavior that does not allow the woman to be a victim. By the end of this book, you will know the steps to conquer any Overwhelming Fear.

She Bear

Chapter 4

Step 1: Listen to Your Inner Sense of Danger

Men are physically stronger and more aggressive than women. However, women are smarter and endowed with a strong sixth sense that, when used to its fullest, helps keep them safe. The problem is that many women suppress this gift because of learned behavior and acquired value that a 21st century woman should not rely on intuition. I call this gift your Inner Sense of Danger. I advise women to learn to use this gift to its full potential in order to avoid danger.

Many women doubt they have this sixth sense or inner power to avoid the danger of becoming a victim. Let me challenge that thought. As you are reading this, imagine that you are seated alone in a room with a door behind you. Picture in your mind's eye that I silently enter the door and stare at you.

What is your reaction? You would turn around and look at me, right? You didn't hear me. You didn't smell me. You didn't taste me. You didn't touch me. You didn't see me. But you knew I was there. Why? It was the Inner Sense of Danger each woman has within her.

Perhaps you have encountered a terrifying experience in the past. I am willing to bet that if I debriefed you regarding the experience, you would explain simply that you "knew" or felt something was wrong, but for whatever reason, you went forward into the danger zone without heeding your inner voice. That was your Disbelief taking over. Believe me, you are not alone. Every female victim I have talked to relates the same thought – "I knew there was something wrong." It was their Inner Sense of Danger warning them. Not listening to the sense is often very costly. Use the gift. God gave it to you for a reason.

Secret Service agents have the enormous task of protecting the President of the United States – a man whose job requires him to be in the public eye, a man who receives hundreds of death threats. The agents keep him safe, not by mowing down everyone in sight or isolating him from the public, but by being alert and avoiding dangerous situations. If something doesn't feel right – perhaps only that some guy looks at the President in a strange way, or someone says something hostile – they move him out. They get him to safety. Secret Service agents, like police, have received extensive training to help them recognize potential dangers. They have honed their sense of danger into a fine instrument. You can, too. You just need to listen for the signals. This book will describe the tools you can hone to be able to effectively listen to your Inner Sense of Danger.

My goal is to help you develop your Inner Sense of Danger to keep you safe and avoid the people or things that may hurt you. This is the first step on your path to becoming a "She Bear" and overcoming Disbelief, Disorientation and Overwhelming Fear.

She Bear

Chapter 5

Step 2: Change Your Mindset

On December 9, 1969, I was made a sergeant squad leader with the Los Angeles Police Department's newly formed Special Weapons and Tactics Unit (SWAT). Shortly before dawn we raided the Los Angeles headquarters of the Black Panther Party in search of illegal weapons and two members who were wanted on assault charges. The raid, which was supposed to be an in-and-out event, resulted in a four-hour gun battle between heavily armed Panthers and approximately 100 police officers trying very hard to utilize military tactics in a police situation. The Panthers barricaded themselves inside a building at 41st Place and Central Avenue in South Central Los Angeles.

The Panthers walked away with some minor injuries that day, but the police officers walked away with an invaluable education. We learned that if SWAT were to be effective, we would have to change our mindset. We needed to rethink our entire approach to law enforcement. We needed more discipline, better organization and a heck of a lot more training.

Five years later, on May 16, 1974, I was working as a lieutenant watch commander at Newton Division for the LAPD. This was the day members of the Symbionese Liberation Army (SLA) entered "Mel's Sporting Goods" in Inglewood, California, and attempted to shoplift several items. When the store security guard stopped them, one of the SLA members brandished a revolver. The security guard knocked it from his hand, and Patty Hearst – who was seated in a van across the street – began shooting into the store with a submachine gun. Hearst, granddaughter of publishing magnate William Randolph Hearst, was an American newspaper heiress and occasional actress. Hearst is an example of a woman who did not fight back to the extreme and actually joined her attackers in their crimes. Hearst's cohorts escaped on foot and took refuge in an Inglewood apartment. When the FBI raided the residence, the suspects disappeared. A van used by the SLA members was abandoned in an alley near 54th Street and Compton Avenue. With as many officers as we could muster, we scoured the neighborhood. As the division lieutenant, I was directed to establish a command post and serve as Incident Commander of the uniformed officers.

An African American woman approached an officer directing traffic and asked what the police planned to do with all the people carrying guns. Assuming the woman was referring to police, the officer assured her the situation was safe and under control. Then, the woman asked: "But what do you plan to do with the women holding guns?" Knowing there were no female police officers on the scene, the officer realized the woman was talking about something else and they had a lead. The elderly woman showed the officer the house with the women holding guns, and the SWAT unit was able to zero in. A gun battle ensued.

Two hours later, when it was over, five SLA members had either been shot or killed in the fire that enflamed the house. Despite the outcome, those of us involved with SWAT saw what a difference five years of training to a new mindset could make. The officers were more disciplined, better organized and more effective. We had changed our mindset and had become better able to control the situation and keep our team safe.

Of course, changing one's mindset is easier said than done, but it can make all the difference in the world. When I was commanding officer of the LAPD's Detective Support Division, I had to appear before a review board to testify after one of my detectives was involved in a fatal shooting with some bank robbers. The bandits – a man and a woman – parked their getaway car in a carport, walked about a block to the bank, donned masks, entered the bank, robbed it, then high-tailed it back to their car. The detectives confronted the robbers at their getaway car, and the male robber was killed in the ensuing shootout. While I addressed the review board, one of the panel members asked why the detectives didn't just disable the getaway car when the robbers headed into the bank. Taht could have prevented the robbers from getting away without using deadly force.

It seemed like a reasonable question, and I didn't have an answer. On return to headquarters, I went to talk to Detective

Bob Richards, senior detective of the Special Investigations Section dedicated to tailing bank robbers and other suspected criminals. "Richy," I said, entering his office, "when we are tailing bandits, why don't we disable their ride when they go into the bank?" Richy lowered his glasses, looked over the rim and said, "What if they don't rob the bank?"

Bandits are skittish folks. They case banks and often are frightened off by some mundane observation they make, or they decide it just does not feel right for "the job." Police can't disable the vehicle of someone they suspect *might be thinking* about committing a crime. Richy's simple observation taught me a lot – about law enforcement and about the criminal mind. After four decades of police work, I have gathered a wealth of knowledge about human behavior and how people operate under stress. I know that just because a bank robber walks into a bank, there is no guarantee he will rob it. And I know that just because a woman is trapped in a seemingly impossible situation, she is not necessarily doomed to be a victim.

Let me share another bank robbery story. When Special Investigations Section was working bank robberies in the early 1980s, they followed a known bandit. They tailed him to a bank in South Central Los Angeles, and watched him park, get out of his car and enter the bank. This criminal was a genius, a real brainchild. He decided he needed a mask for this operation, so he pulled out a paper bag as he entered the bank and put it over his head. Instead of cutting eyeholes, as you might expect, this guy cut a face hole. There he was, walking up to the teller, saying, "Give me your money!" with his entire face poking through the hole in the paper bag like one of those wooden photo op stations you see at amusement parks. Needless to say, the bank teller didn't have much difficulty identifying the robber!

The point of these stories I have shared is that the average criminal is dumb and skittish. The slightest bit of resistance will send him looking for another victim. Always remember that even though an attacker has an advantage over you when it comes to height, weight and physical strength, you will always be smarter than your attacker.

She Bear

Chapter 6

Smarts Winning Over Strength

When I was commanding officer of the West Los Angeles Division in 1992, I learned of an unusual call. A woman was home alone in her apartment. She closed the blinds and hopped into the shower to get ready to go out for the evening. When she got out of the shower, she toweled off and walked naked into her kitchen to grab a glass of water. When she got to the living room, a man was standing there, watching her.

Somehow, this man entered her apartment. He intended to rape her. He grabbed the woman and started to unbutton his pants. The woman had no clothes and no weapon, but she was not defenseless. She told the would-be rapist she was not about to have unprotected sex with him but if he went down to the corner liquor store and got some condoms, she would be happy to have sex with him. Thinking it was his lucky day, the guy buttoned his pants, stepped out the front door and headed for the store. Guess who was waiting for him when he returned? The woman was not defenseless.

Armed with nothing but a superior intellect, that young woman refused to be a victim that day. She refused to submit to the Disbelief, Disorientation and Overwhelming Fear. And she won. Needless to say, she now locks her doors when home alone.

Society teaches women – and this is especially true for older generations – to be submissive. There is a stereotype that women have to be nice and polite. Sometimes, that niceness can lead to submissiveness, which can lead to victimization. I give you all license to be rude when confronted with a situation that causes your Inner Sense of Danger to alert. Act the part, speak the part, and *refuse* to be a victim.

Most readers have probably seen the *Rocky* movies starring Sylvester Stallone. In the first *Rocky*, there is a scene where Talia Shire'a character, Adrian, is in a pet store buying a turtle. She is wearing a long frumpy coat and a floppy hat, no makeup, and an expression that makes her appear afraid of her own shadow. Sylvester Stallone's character, Rocky, starts to flirt with her, and Adrian is beside herself. She doesn't know what to say or do. It's clear she wants to get away from the big lug, but she is too meek and polite to do so. Fast forward to the following Rocky movies in which Adrian is the dynamic, charismatic wife of a boxing superstar. There is a scene where Adrian is walking down the street, fashionably dressed, head up, shoulders back, a little strut in her walk. Hair: perfect. Makeup: perfect. She's a head turner. If I show those two pictures of Adrian to dozens of convicts, they will all say the same thing. The first Adrian – the frumpy 'fraidy cat" – fits the profile of a rape victim. Why? It's about attitude. It's about changing your mindset and projecting the message that you are not a victim.

A few years ago, I gave the "She Bear" presentation to a group of women in Orange County, California. One of the women in the class came up to me afterward and asked what she should do about some laborers who sometimes worked for the business she and her husband operate together. The laborers often stood in front of a door she exited to move between buildings on her property. She said the workers made her uncomfortable when she passed by them. She had the feeling they were undressing her with their eyes. I told her to walk right up to them, look them in the eye and say, "Good morning. Thank you all for being here. My husband and I really appreciate your presence here." Then walk away. She called me later and said she had done it. She walked up to the guys with her heart stomping like crazy. She could barely get the words out, but she took a deep breath, looked each one in the eye and established her dominance. She made it clear that she would not be intimidated by their presence. That woman overcame her Disbelief, Disorientation and Overwhelming Fear, and she confronted her intimidators. She was like the head-turner Adrian from the later Rocky film. She adopted the attitude and projected the message that she was in charge. She dominated the situation.

Sometimes, however, it requires more than attitude. Sometimes, you have to shock them with what you say and how you say it.

It's a rare occasion when a crook just grabs a woman and assaults her. He almost always tests the waters with an innocuous-sounding question or gentle touch. The No. 1 question: "Hey, lady, do you have the time?" In the instant it takes for a woman to register the question, look down at her watch, and answer, the crook will size her up – is this a frog or a She Bear? As I said before, criminals are skittish. They prefer the path of least resistance. Just as a bank robber cases the bank before pulling the stickup, a rapist cases his victim to determine whether she is likely to fight him.

The female propensity for politeness often takes over here. Women almost always want to be helpful and answer the question. But, if you are alone – perhaps walking to your car or jogging down the street – change your mindset and resist the temptation. If your Inner Sense of Danger alerts, listen to it. Don't pause. Don't look down at your watch. Don't even break your stride. Just look the guy straight in the eye and say, "Fuck you! Buy a watch." And keep moving.

If what I am telling you sounds harsh and you think you could never do it, consider the story of a grandmother who sat through my "She Bear" presentation a few years back. A few months after the presentation, she called to thank me. She had been in the car with her daughter and 2-year-old granddaughter one day. The daughter, who was driving, pulled into a 7-Eleven and ran inside to get some milk for the baby. While the grandmother was sitting in the running car, a man jumped into the driver's seat and said, "Hang on, grandma, we're going for a ride." This woman – who was straight out of central casting for the role of a sweet old granny in a television show – shouted, "Fuck you! Get out of my car." And he did. The woman was so shocked that she had used that language, but I imagine the crook was more shocked. With those seven words and stern tone, the elderly woman established her dominance, and was able to keep herself and her baby granddaughter from being victims that day.

I have shared a lot of stories and anecdotes with you in this chapter, but they all have one purpose: to help you realize that you can change your mindset. It took the LAPD's SWAT team five years and several hundred rounds of ammunition to figure out that we needed to change the way we practice law enforcement. The process will be much easier for you, I promise. Listen to your Inner Sense of Danger. Use your superior intellect. Put your head up, shoulders back, and look your intimidators straight in the eye.

Don't be afraid to use shocking language and a loud voice to convey to a would-be attacker that you will not be made to feel afraid. Above all, remember the sweet grandmother fighting to protect herself and her granddaughter. The She Bear fighting to protect something precious will always prevail over the dumb, skittish criminal.

She Bear

Chapter 7

Situations to Avoid

The Elevator

Picture that you are alone in a building after hours, waiting for an elevator. The elevator arrives, the door opens and a man is standing inside alone. Your sense of danger lights up. Alert, alert, alert. Does it make any sense to enter the elevator? No, it does not. However, most women will enter the elevator putting them in harm's way. Why? They figure that the sense of danger is wrong or weak. They don't want to appear rude or crazy for not getting into the elevator when it arrives. Is it really worth the risk? React to your Inner Sense of Danger and walk away or point down the hall as if you see someone and leave. You can act like you forgot something at your office and walk toward other people. If your sense of danger tells you not to get on that elevator, listen to it: Do not get on the elevator.

Here's another scenario: the elevator arrives, the man is alone, but you don't sense danger. Perhaps he looks friendly or you have seen him before around the building. You get in the elevator. Now, there is an unwritten protocol for how strangers should act on elevators. A man knows that the woman is uncomfortable. Therefore, he might say hello, but make no further attempts at conversation. The normal thing to do is stand on opposite sides and silently watch the numbers over the door as the elevator passes floors. This is standard behavior. Any deviation from this protocol should cause your sense of danger to ring emergency bells. If this happens, you need to take control and establish that you will not be a victim. I discuss this in more depth later in the book, but the abridged version is this: look him in the eye, put your head up, shoulders back, summon your most dominant voice, and get ready to go on the offensive using the head butt or testicle-grabbing techniques (See Chapter 8).

The Parking Lot or Garage

You are at the mall, the stores are closing and you are returning to your parked car. It is dark, and you have a long distance to walk. You don't see or hear anything that gives you pause, but your sense of danger lights up. What do you do? Many women will ignore the feeling and walk to their car with no consequence. But is it worth the risk? Walk back inside the store; ask a clerk, security guard or another shopper to walk you to your car. If you really can't bring yourself to ask for help, wait for other shoppers who are walking to their cars, and follow them out the door. This is a simple and effective safety move.

Scams

There are many scams would-be attackers use to lure women into a trap. Emily was driving into a well-lit gas station at around 9:30 p.m. Because she had attended one of my lectures she looked around her environment before stepping out of the car. Her Inner Sense of Danger was alerted and she was able to follow it. She noticed two large, tough looking men loitering around the gas station without a car. She also noticed a white car in the un-lit area of the gas station.

When she got out of her car, she continued to use her Inner Sense of Danger and be aware of her surroundings, even though there were many other drivers filling their gas tanks. While she was filling up her car, a clean-cut man who looked like he was in his twenties approached her and asked her if she'd like to sample a perfume and that he had more in the trunk of his car. Right away, she knew this was a set up and yelled at the man, "Get away from me!" He responded by saying, in a calm voice, "I just thought you might like to test some of our samples." Again, Emily yelled "Get away from me!" The clean-cut man walked away and went back to his car.

As soon as the man had approached her, Emily knew the writing on the wall. If she had gone over to the trunk and smelled the "perfume" she would have become unconscious and the two large, tough looking men would have most likely pushed her into the trunk.

The first thing she did was to go into the gas station and tell the attendant what was going on and that he needed to call the police to get the men out of the gas station. He replied in a casual manner, "Oh, yeah, they've been here a few times before."

Outraged, Emily questioned the attendant on why he had not called the police and angrily told the man, "You need to call the police and tell them what's going on and call them again if they continue to show-up."

The gas store attendant lazily said he would call the police. Unbelieving the man, she turned and went back to her car, locked the doors and drove away. As she was driving home she called 911 and relayed the situation. Officers were able to come out and take care of the situation. When you are faced with what your Inner Sense of Danger is telling you is a scam, don't trust that it is being taken care of. Call the police and notify the women in your life of the situation you encountered so that they may avoid a similar hoax.

The Uninvited Guest

You're home alone or with your children. It's 8 p.m. and well after dark. The doorbell rings. You are not expecting anyone. Your sense of danger alerts. You don't have to answer the door. It might be just a neighbor or friend stopping by, but is it worth the risk to open the door not knowing who is there? Look through the peephole, look out a window and ask through the door, "Who's there?" But don't open the door. Your sense of danger may know something that your conscious mind does not know. Listen to it.

Walking Alone

You are walking or jogging alone down the street. A man whom you do not know begins to take an unusual interest in you. Maybe he switches direction and follows you. Maybe he just looks at you in a strange way. Whatever it is, something about him causes your Inner Sense of Danger to go off. What do you do? Is it your instinct to look him straight in the eye? Cross the street? Duck into a store? Walk toward other people? These are preventative actions. You should do something that lets him know you see him, and something about him bothers you. To become a She Bear, you must listen to your Inner Sense of Danger. If a criminal's intentions are evil, he likely will get skittish and walk away. If you're feeling was wrong, the worse that can happen is you've interrupted your morning jog or you need to circle back to your car. Practice these safety tips when you know you are safe for the times you will need to use them: when your Inner Sense of Danger is alerted.

She Bear

Chapter 8

Simple Safety Techniques

In the previous chapters I presented two critical concepts about listening to your Inner Sense of Danger and changing your mindset. By doing these two things, you will be 80% safer. The next step is to introduce a few simple, active techniques that will further increase your safety.

Scan the Room

I cannot reinforce enough that the best way to stay safe is to avoid dangerous situations. Listening to your Inner Sense of Danger is part of this process, but there is another component: be aware of your environment. When you walk into a room, look around. Take a quick glance at who is there. See what they are doing. Notice how they are dressed. Look at their expressions. Ask yourself the question: does anything seem out of place? For instance, if the clerk behind the counter at the convenience store has a strange look on his face, consider whether there is a robbery in progress. If there are men in heavy, bulky jackets and it's the middle of summer, consider whether they have guns hiding under all that bulk.

Many stores and restaurants have glass doors or windows in front. Before you enter, look inside. If it is a bank, look to see whether anyone is holding a gun or wearing a mask. The last thing you want to do is walk into the middle of a bank robbery. Furthermore, if you decide to enter the room or building, look for the exits. If things go awry, you want to know how to escape quickly. Too often, people get trampled or killed by stacking up at the exits trying to get out when danger hits.

If scanning the room seems a little too cloak-and-dagger, consider the costs versus the benefits. It only takes a few seconds to look through the window or look around a room, but the benefits to you in terms of safety are immeasurable. Imagine how comfortable you will feel knowing you were alert and have an exit plan.

Pepper Spray

Women often ask me if they should get a gun for protection. Although I carry a pistol and all of my officers carry a firearm, I discourage women from buying a gun unless they plan to get the certified training they will need to use it safely and effectively. All too often, women and men who pull a gun on their attacker hesitate before pulling the trigger, and that second of self-doubt allows the attacker to grab the gun and use it on the gun owner. The other downside of a gun is that you cannot carry it with you unless you have a special concealed weapon permit, which is very difficult to obtain – especially in California. That means the gun you spent hundreds of dollars to purchase and the hours of training you underwent will be useless to you if an attacker grabs you on the street or in a shopping mall parking lot.

Instead, I have two words for you: *oleoresin capsicum* (OC). OC is the reddish oil extracted from chili peppers, which gives them their hot quality. Chemists have been able to turn the OC extract into a liquid self-defense spray. OC, or "pepper spray" as it is commonly called, inflames an attacker's mucous membranes (eyes, nose, throat and lungs) immediately upon contact. He will be temporarily blinded, and will usually fall to the ground gasping for breath. He will forget all about attacking you in his quest for water and air, and you will have time to get away or take control of the situation.

I recommend you purchase a canister of OC (pepper spray), which costs only about $5 to $10. Look for the 10% formulation, and be sure to get the stream rather than the spray; it deploys like a squirt gun, making it easy to control. It is very important to read the instructions. When you buy the canister, be sure you know how to activate the spray. Keep it with you at all times. They now make pepper spray to fit in your purse, your pocket, or on your key chain. They even make a canister that looks like a lipstick. Always keep your pepper spray in the same spot so you don't have to think about where it is should the need arise. If you keep it in your purse, take it out whenever you are walking alone and carry it in your free hand, ready to use. Carry keys, bags, drinks, or other items, in your other hand so you won't have to juggle the pepper spray canister if you need to spray it at an attacker. Keep in mind that pepper spray has a lifespan of five years.

Pepper spray is readily available in sporting goods stores and from online retailers. In most states you do not need a permit or special training to carry it. Note, however, that New York has very strict rules about obtaining and carrying pepper spray. Children under 18 and convicted felons may not carry pepper spray in New York, and New Yorkers who are allowed to carry it must fill out a registration form when they purchase it. Additionally, airlines do not permit you to bring the spray on the plane in your carry-on luggage. Currently the Federal Transportation Security Administration permits passengers to pack a small (4 fl. oz. can) of pepper spray in their checked luggage if the canister is equipped with a security latch to prevent accidental discharge. For more information on traveling with pepper spray online, go to www.tsa.gov.

Should you ever need to use your pepper spray, try to stand two or three feet away from your attacker for maximum effect. Direct it toward his face, and spray a stream into his eyes, nose and mouth. Then run away and get help. Do not watch to see if it works – assume it will work and run.

Head Butt

As you may have guessed from the previous discussion about pepper spray, I believe in resistance. If you are attacked, be a She Bear and fight to the death. Hit, scratch, bite, or scream. Do whatever you need to, but do not ever let an assailant take you to another location. If he promises not to hurt you, he's lying. If he wants to move you, it's because he wants to rape you and/or kill you. A lot of books on self-defense discuss complicated techniques that involve martial arts or using your keys as a weapon. For some women these techniques may be helpful, but I believe in using your head – literally!

If an attacker grabs you from the front and you don't have your pepper spray, let him get just close enough, then smash him with your forehead. Aim for that spot between his eyes and imagine that you are Brandi Chastain or Mia Hamm attempting to knock a soccer ball into the goal. Swing your neck forward and give him a head butt that will send him reeling. Even if it doesn't knock him unconscious or break his nose, it will definitely shock him, and you will have a few precious moments to get away.

Grab his Testicles

The last technique I want to discuss is one near and dear to every man's heart. Any woman who has ever borne a child knows the intense pain of childbirth. It's something you could never convey in words to any man, but it's something you probably will never forget. Now, imagine inflicting that kind of pain on an attacker. There is a way to do it: Grab his testicles.

Women who have been raped remember feeling the fear, the pain, and the helplessness. More than anything else, the victims recall their attacker's hot, bad breath in their face. The breath is always there. But, what else is always there during a rape? His testicles. Whether he threatens you with a gun, a knife or just his brute strength, there will always be a moment when his testicles are exposed. That is your moment. Grab his testicles and twist and pull as hard as you can. Imagine that you are back in grade school playing tug-of-war over a pit of mud. Someone is going into that mud and you don't want it to be you. Grab, squeeze, twist and pull with all your might, and I promise you will win. He will double over in pain and fall to the ground, and you will get your chance to escape.

Chapter 9

Home Safety

On June 28, 1984, a man named Richard Ramirez slipped into the ground-floor apartment of 79-year-old Jennie Vincow. She had left a window open because it was hot that night. Ramirez simply removed the screen and climbed inside. He ransacked her apartment, sexually assaulted her and then stabbed her in the throat so brutally he nearly decapitated her. During the next year, Ramirez entered dozens of other homes in Los Angeles, Orange and San Francisco counties. He often shot the husband in the head, raped and murdered the wife, then ransacked the house for any valuables he could sell. He usually struck in the middle of the night while families were sleeping, and he left behind vestiges of his Satan worship. Thus, he earned the media moniker "Night Stalker."

Ramirez often entered through open windows and unlocked doors. Sometimes, he cut a window screen to ease his entry. Between March and August of 1985, newspapers, radio, and TV news broadcasts chronicled the Night Stalker's rampage through frightened neighborhoods. But, despite the public awareness and the fear, Ramirez still was able to reach many of his victims through unsecured doors and windows.

Lock Doors and Windows

This is not rocket science; the easiest, most effective way to ensure your safety at home is to lock your doors and windows. If you need to open your windows when it is warm, install safety latches that allow you to open the window part way, but prevent someone from pushing it all the way open from the outside and entering the house. Sliding glass doors often have a safety pin that allows you to open the door a few inches for air, while keeping the door secure against intruders. This is an inexpensive and effective safety mechanism. If you like to open your front door for air or visibility, consider installing a security screen that you can lock to keep out burglars. Just make sure you can unlock the door quickly in case of fire or other emergency.

Don't Open for Strangers

Home invasion robberies are the new fad in the criminal world. A group of hoodlums ring a doorbell and force their way inside when the door is opened. They terrorize the family and ransack the house, looking for cash and valuables. Then they walk out the front door and drive away.

Although I mentioned this in Chapter 7, it bears repeating: If you don't know the person at your door, don't open the door. Ask his or her business while the door is closed and locked. If he claims he's from the gas or water company and there is a leak, ask for a phone number you can call to verify his legitimacy. If your door does not already have one, install a peephole. They cost only about $5 at the hardware store, and require a drill and a few minutes of your time to install. The peace of mind you get from knowing who is there before you open the door will make it time well spent. If you don't have a peephole, make it your practice to determine who is at your front door before you unlock and open the door.

After you determine who is at the door and ask what they want, if your Inner Sense of Danger alerts, don't open the door. Tell them through the door that you are busy and will not open the door. The worse that can happen is that he will think you are rude. If it's a delivery, he will either leave it on your porch or require you to pick it up at the Fed Ex or UPS office. But, if the person intends to harm you, and you do not open the door, you have just made it that much more difficult for him to reach you. Chances are good that he will leave you alone and look for another victim. Sometimes, the "She Bear" wins by knowing how and when to avoid the battle.

Get a Dog

Imagine you are a burglar looking for a house to rob. Do you approach the one with the dog in the yard? Even if the dog is not ferocious looking, the threat of barking will cause a burglar to keep moving. If you don't already have one, get a dog. A dog is a great companion. A dog will die for you without any training. If something happens to you, that dog will lie down beside you, whimper and cry until help arrives. In addition to keeping you company, a dog has incredible senses and will be very protective of you. The best dog, in my opinion, is a female German Shepard. Even without training, she will be a very loyal and excellent guard dog.

Get an Alarm

Many people think of home alarms as something they turn on when they leave the house in order to protect against a burglar slipping in when they are gone. Often people don't know that home alarms also have a nighttime mode that can be set for protection when you are at home. The alarm alerts the residents when a door or window is opened, but does not sound off when you walk around the house. Although an alarm system can be pricey, once you pay the installation fee and monthly service charge, some home insurance companies will lower your rate if you have an alarm system. Additionally, the peace of mind gained from having the alarm system can make it worth the financial cost.

Create a Safe Room

So, you have locked the doors, locked the windows, installed a peephole, gotten a dog and bought an alarm. But, you still feel a little nervous when you are home alone. I recommend that you turn your bedroom into a safe room.

Unlike your front door, most bedroom doors are hollow core. They are intended for privacy, not security. But, that is easily changed. Go to your hardware store and purchase a solid core front door and have it installed on your bedroom. Next, put a deadbolt on the new door to provide extra security. Make sure the windows in your bedroom lock securely. Of course, you need to make sure you can get out of your room and out of the house quickly in case of emergency, but consider this your cocoon of safety. Finally, the most important element in your safe room is a cell phone. Keep it charged, keep it near your bed, and make sure you get reception at your house. If you hear someone breaking into your house at night, your cell phone is your connection to the police. Program 911 into your phone or better yet as a speed dial. Read your manual to see if there is an auto speed dial. And the greatest thing about cell phones? Nobody can cut the line like they do in the old movies!

She Bear

Chapter 10

Car Safety

There's a saying that Americans live in their cars. If you have a long commute to work or you spend a good portion of your day picking up children and dropping them off at school and sports practice, you probably see the truth in that cliché. Despite all of the time we spend in our cars, however, most people don't give much thought to assure their safety while in their vehicles.

Lock the Doors

The simplest safety measure you can adopt is to lock your doors the minute you get into the car. Some of the newer cars automatically lock the doors when the car is put into gear; you can be even more proactive. Lock your car doors immediately. That way, if you sit in your car for a moment to look for directions, play with the radio or wait for a passenger, no one will be able to hop into the car with you. Additionally, if you are one of those people who balances the checkbook in the car after shopping or going to the bank, break that habit now. You should approach your car with keys in hand, unlock the door, get inside, close the door, lock it, and drive away. The less time you spend sitting alone in your parked car in a parking lot or garage reduces the amount of time a criminal will have to make you a victim.

Roll Up Windows

Second only to the unlocked door, the open window is the easiest way for a criminal to get at you in the car. You can easily close off that pathway by rolling up your window. If you don't have air conditioning and you really need to let some air into the car, roll down the window a few inches – enough for the air to get in, but not enough for a would-be carjacker's hand to reach into your car to grab you or unlock your car door.

Carry a Cell Phone

Vandalism and maintenance costs have resulted in fewer and fewer pay telephones being available in public places, making it less likely that you will find a pay phone when you need it. Additionally, the call boxes on highways in some states can be helpful in case of car trouble, but sometimes they are broken or require a long walk on an unsafe stretch of road. These are being phased out due to extensive cell phone use. Therefore, I urge you to buy a cell phone and carry it with you for emergencies. If your car breaks down, you run out of gas, get lost or get in an accident, that cell phone will be your best friend. If you are a technophobe like myself, learn to conquer that fear and have someone show you how to use it. As a police officer,

I have seen a lot of highway kidnappings that could have been prevented if the motorist had a cell phone to call for help.

Stop 1½ Car Lengths Behind the Limit Line

Another car safety technique that never occurred to me until I started doing "She Bear" presentations in Southern California has to do with stopping for a red light or stop sign. I have heard women complain about men in nearby cars who leer and make obscene gestures at women driving alone. The solution for this problem is simple: if you are the first person to pull to the limit line at a red light, stop your car several feet – or about 1½ car lengths – back from the intersection. The person in the lane next to you will likely pull to the line, and you will not be eye to eye. Your cars will be staggered, and it will be more difficult for him to look back over his shoulder and make you uncomfortable. If the car in the lane next to you has already stopped when you pull up to the red light, position your car so that your windows do not line up. In the 1960s the Oakland Police Department adopted this staggered-position practice after members of the Black Panther Party planned ambushes on officers. This technique reduced the opportunity for the menacing cross look, and it kept officers safer. It will work for you, too.

Being Followed? Make Three Right Turns

Most of us drive by rote. Deep in thought, we often reach our destination without ever having experienced the trip. Starting at point A, and driving to point D, we do not recall passing points B or C. This is very common, and will always be with us. But if you are alone in your car, you especially need to be aware of your environment. Try this tactic: during the last three blocks before you reach your destination, shake off the trance. Look in the rear-view mirror and see who is around you. If you think a car may be following you, make three right turns. If the suspected car makes those right turns, too, don't drive home. Go straight to a police station, or any place where there are people and light. The person following you will likely give up and look for another victim. Try to get the license plate number and physical description of the car's occupants, and notify the police.

Cause a Crash if Necessary

Here is another scenario: you are at a red light, and a man walks through the stopped traffic and approaches your car with a gun or knife. If you are the first car in line, drive off. The worst that can happen is you cause an accident. An accident means honking horns, police sirens and lots of attention – exactly what the criminal does not want. If you are not the first car at the intersection, and other cars are blocking you in, begin to honk your horn and yell for help. By causing a commotion, you will call attention to yourself and scare off the criminal. If that gun-toting thug thought he was going to victimize a fearful frog, he'll get a crash-course in the ways of the "She Bear."

Find a Well-Lit Place to Exchange Accident Information

Now, this is a favorite tactic of attackers and carjackers: they cause a minor fender-bender with a woman who is alone in her car, then they victimize her when she gets out to exchange information. Of course, the vehicle code tells us all that we cannot leave the scene of an accident, and that we need to exchange information for insurance purposes. Just remember, you don't have to get out of your car to exchange information. If it is nighttime and/or you are in an area with few people, keep your windows up and your doors locked. You can exchange information through a crack in your window. Or, better yet, tell the other driver to follow you to a well-lit place nearby where there are lots of people – a police station if possible. You can exchange information there and use your cell phone to notify someone where you are and why you will be delayed. Meanwhile, note his license plate and car description in case he drives away. That way, you can file with your insurance company for any damage done during the crash.

Jump Out if Necessary

Finally, I want to talk about something that will be very difficult if you ever have to do it, but it could mean the difference between life and death. Even if you always roll up your windows, lock your doors, stop back from the limit line, and drive away, there is still a chance that you will be held against your will in an automobile. If approached by an attacker, there may come a day when someone is able to breach the safety of your vehicle and enter your car. If this should ever happen, you must jump out of the car. These rules apply whether the assailant forces you to drive him in your car, or he pulls you into his car. Don't be lulled into thinking that if you just go along with him, everything will be fine. If an attacker wants to move you, chances are good that he wants to rape you or kill you. I have never seen a situation where things got better for a victim who was taken in a car. The situation always gets worse. You must do whatever it takes to get away; you must get out of the car.

Here's how: watch the speedometer; at some point, the car will have to slow for a stop sign, red light or turn. When the car is traveling less than 15 miles per hour, ask the kidnapper a question. As he answers, open the door and jump. Don't try to stay on your feet. Just land on your feet, tuck your head under your arms, drop to the ground and roll. Be ready to experience some pain. You likely will be scraped up and possibly suffer broken bones, but it will be a lot better than the alternative. The car will keep moving down the street, and you will have a chance to get to safety.

I am often asked what a woman should do if she has a child in the car. My answer is the same. Jump out and get to safety. You are your child's best hope for being rescued. The attacker most likely wants you – not the child. If you remain in the car, your child's chances decline. If you jump out, you will be able to call the police and allow them to save your baby.

I know this may sound a little like Starsky and Hutch, but I promise it will work. My best friend, Bob Smitson, and I trained narcotics officers who often found themselves in some pretty sticky situations. This jump-and-roll maneuver was one of the tactics we trained officers to use. A young undercover officer was operating with narcotics dealers. The suspects' leaders intended to rob the officer rather than sell narcotics.

This was a "rip." The dealers planned to steal from the officer and kill him. One of the guys in the front seat stuck a .45 caliber pistol into the officer's side. Another one in the back seat put a sawed off rifle to his head. The dealer in the passenger's seat had another pistol pointed at the floor of the car. The officer was young, but he was no novice. He knew what those guys planned to do, and he knew he had to get out of that car.

As he drove to a location where cover officers were located, the undercover officer made the decision to jump. At about 10 miles per hour, he opened the door and rolled to the ground. The car kept moving. One shot went into the floorboard. Another shot went through the windshield. And the third shot went through the open door, and missed the officer who was lying on the pavement. The reason that officer escaped without being shot is because those drug dealers were hindered by their reaction time.

Reaction time is the one or two seconds it takes every human to process what is happening, develop a response and act. You may recall your driver's training or physics class in high school when the instructor talked about the amount of time it takes a person to stop a car in an emergency. There is a lag time between when the brain perceives the need to stop and the time it takes to complete the physical action of moving your foot from the gas pedal to the brake. Professional quarterbacks, fighter pilots and racecar drivers have some of the fastest reaction times – probably about a half second. The rest of us require a few seconds to think and act. If you decide to open the car door and jump out, you get the benefit of developing the plan in your own head while your kidnapper is focused on something else. When you physically open the door and jump, the kidnapper must react to your action, which gives you a second or two to drop to the ground and roll before he is able to pull the trigger and/or grab the steering wheel. One or two seconds in that fast-moving situation is a long time. Take advantage of it to get to safety.

Chapter 11

Date Rape

One of the most difficult crimes for police to investigate and for district attorneys to prosecute is date rape. The case often comes down to a "he-said/she-said" dispute between the victim and the attacker. We often see cases involving 16- or 17-year-old boys who either misread the signals or ignored explicit pleas to stop, and young women who feel ashamed that they didn't do more to make it stop.

Often, a young woman will dress as pretty as she can to go out on a date with high expectations that everything will go well, and that she will have a good time. Meanwhile, young men have similar hopes that things will go well, but they have different ideas about what constitutes a good time. The guy often thinks: if I can, I will. I like to compare young men to search dogs. The dog is motivated to search by the possibility of a fight. The young man is motivated to date by the possibility of having sex.

When kissing leads to fondling and you are ready for things to stop, you must never forget that you are in charge of your own body. When you want things to stop, you must tell the guy, and he has to respect it. If you do not want things to go any further, you must control your own hormones and desires and be clear with the young man. Saying no very forcefully will make a guy back off 90% of the time, and that will be the end of it.

However, if he does not stop when you say no, but continues to force sex, the best advice I can give is this: bite him on the cheek as hard as you can. I guarantee that will stop the encounter. If not, we no longer have a "he-said/she-said." We have evidence of forcible rape, and you should report it to the police as soon as possible.

A police officer's goal is to find the truth. Unfortunately, we often get complaints of rape where it is clear that sexual intercourse occurred, but the man claims it was consensual, and we have no bruises, scrapes, or cuts to prove it wasn't consensual. Also, date rape cases usually are reported hours or days later, further eroding the evidence. A woman who has been raped often feels very dirty and the first thing she does is take a shower washing away evidence and making an investigator's job all the more difficult.

The victim advocate for the Fullerton Police Department, Dody Rehrer, often meets with women who have been raped to try to help them get over the trauma and shock. When Rehrer sits with the victim in an emergency room the young girl invariably express denial, disbelief and anger. The young woman also often conveys a feeling of shame, a disconnection from her body and frozen from the situation. They want so badly to do something to make the man understand that what he did was wrong. They quickly find out, however, that the process of investigating a rape is more difficult for the victim than the attacker. Women have to undergo a physical examination that can feel as degrading as the rape itself. The investigative questions require her to relive the entire experience. And her past sexual experiences often are dragged into the case.

In her 11 years with my department, Dody has met with more than 500 victims of sexual assault and domestic violence. She has seen more cases be dropped from a lack of evidence than prosecuted. She says a woman's reaction when a case is dropped is almost always the same: "What could I have done?" In the case of rape, my answer is to keep fighting. Don't ever give up and just let the man rape you with no resistance. Try to stop the sexual encounter by saying no, and try to get away. But if he still persists, make him feel your pain – bite, scratch, hit – anything that will leave a sign of your resistance so that we will have evidence when it comes time to arrest and prosecute him.

She Bear

Chapter 12

Stalking

In July of 1990 I was commanding officer of the Los Angeles Police Department SWAT unit. A woman obsessed with actress Sharon Gless from TV's "Cagney and Lacey" entered the star's home with a rifle and 500 rounds of ammunition. Joni Leigh Penn was in love with Gless, and she threatened to kill herself in front of the actress. Fortunately, Gless was not home at the time, and my unit responded before she returned. Obviously, Gless was not about to enter her home and listen to the woman profess her love.

As the commanding officer on scene, I was responsible for developing the plan to get into the house, arrest the woman and get her out. As I was instructing my officers on how to proceed, I received a call from a high-ranking official in the LAPD. He said, "Pat, the person in that house is my niece. She has a lot of problems, but she's a good person. Please don't hurt her." I assured him we would not kill her. We successfully entered the house and arrested Penn before she could harm herself or anyone else. That stalking incident ended peacefully, but unfortunately many situations result in injury or death for one or both parties.

One out of 12 women and one out of 45 men in the United States has been stalked at some point in his or her life, according to the National Violence Against Women Survey published in 1998 by the United States Department of Justice Office and the National Institute of Justice Centers for Disease Control. Almost three-quarters of stalking victims are between the ages of 18- and 39-years-old. Most stalking cases involve perpetrators and victims who know each other; strangers stalk only 23% of all female victims and 36% of all male victims.

California passed the nation's first anti-stalking statute (California Penal Code § 646.9) in 1990. By 1995 every state and the District of Columbia had stalking laws. According to the National Violence Against Women Survey, reports to police by stalking victims increased after 1990. But, many incidents still go unreported; only 55% of female victims and 48% of male victims said their stalking was reported to police. Most stalking victims in the study said they did not report the incident because they did not think it was a police matter. They thought police would not be able to do anything, or feared reprisals from the stalker.

Stalkers' activities include: following their victims, spying on them, standing outside their home or place of work, making unsolicited phone calls, sending unwanted letters or emails, vandalizing their property, and killing or threatening to kill their pets. California law describes a stalker as: "Any person who willfully, maliciously, and repeatedly follows or willfully and maliciously harasses another person and who makes a credible threat with the intent to place that person in reasonable fear for his or her safety, or the safety of his or her immediate family." One of the commanding officers at the Fullerton Police Department has come up with his own definition: "Any sicko who can't control the sick behavior and won't stop bugging someone else, then scares them really bad, gets all happy about scaring them and makes them think they or their family might die." The officer closes his definition with this warning: "If you are stalking, we will be talking."

That warning is important, just as it is important for victims to alert police to what is happening. What may start as annoying phone calls and letters will usually intensify over time, as the stalker gets more and more bold. Involving the police early allows officers to monitor the person, talk to him and determine if a crime has been committed. I am a big believer in the value of having an authoritative figure, such as a police officer, confront the person and advise him that his behavior is unacceptable. Some stalkers will be deterred by the involvement of law enforcement. For those who don't get the message, police officers can help a victim get a restraining order and begin to build a case for future prosecution. Many victims feel better just knowing the number of a detective they can call whenever the person acts offensively.

Too often, victims do not report stalking behavior because they are afraid the stalker will lose his temper. Some authorities disagree with me on this subject, but I believe in confronting stalkers as soon as the unacceptable behavior begins. Placating or ignoring the stalker will only allow him to grow stronger. Take stalkers seriously. Victims should contact their local police agency as early as possible and be guided by the detective's instruction and advice.

Chapter 13

Surviving a Hostage Crisis

Throughout this book, I have talked about the importance of standing tall, being confident and confronting an attacker. There is one situation, however, where the best thing you can do is lay low and submit. A hostage crisis requires the "She Bear" to recognize that she is outnumbered and outgunned. In most hostage situations, the gunmen do not care about you. They just want to get in, get the what they came for and get out. In these cases, resistance will get you killed.

Now, let me be clear about what I mean by a hostage crisis. I am talking about a bank or store robbery or a crazed shooter in the post office, shopping mall or school cafeteria. None of us will ever forget the valor and self-sacrifice of the passengers aboard United Flight 93 whose resistance on September 11, 2001, forced the hijacked plane to crash in a Pennsylvania field instead of a populated area in Washington, D.C.

Resistance was the right course of action that day. However, resistance does not change the outcome of events and will usually be an unnecessary risk.

Lay Low and Play Invisible

When people hear gunshots, their first reaction is to look around to determine the direction, and then they scream and run. This is the worst possible response. Gunmen shoot at movement. Don't be the movement that catches their eye in the confusion. Lie on the ground and be as still as possible – preferably under a table or near a wall so that other people running away do not trample you. This will be very difficult because your first instinct will be to get away. But, I want you to get on the ground and keep telling yourself, "I'm invisible. I'm invisible. I'm invisible." Pretend that you are a little girl playing hide and seek. If you stay still and quiet, all of the commotion will rush past you, and you will remain safe. Don't react. Don't scream. The mind game of being a little girl again will get you through the ordeal. After it's over, you can cry and scream.

Now, when you're in the situation of a bank robbery with armed gunmen shouting orders and merely brandishing weapons – do exactly as you are told. If they say get on the ground, you should get on the ground. Try not to cry. Don't try to be a hero. The worst that will happen is that you may end up with the butt of a shotgun in your face as the gunman tries to establish order. Be prepared for harsh language such as, "Bitch! Shut up!" But, just tell yourself that you can get through it.

Look Them in the Eye

On December 17, 1981, members of the Red Brigade terrorist group kidnapped U.S. Brigadier General James Dozier from his apartment in Verona, Italy. Dozier, the highest ranking NATO official in Italy, was held captive for what seemed like an eternity and eventually rescued by an elite Italian counter-terrorist police unit. The first rescuer on the scene was able to disarm the terrorist guarding Dozier. That terrorist was arrested and questioned along with four other captors. When authorities asked the terrorist why he did not just kill Dozier, he said he had been with the general for several days, and he was no longer the enemy. He said the general had become a real person. That personal connection between Dozier and the terrorist saved Dozier's life. It can save yours too.

Some people say the eyes are the windows to the soul. Let the gunman see into your soul and it will make it that much harder for him to kill you. Just look him in the eye, give him the money, and let him leave. Now, the tactics I have discussed in this chapter apply to bank and store robberies – situations where it is clear that the gunman only wants to get the money and get out. Do not confuse this with being confronted by a rapist or someone else who clearly wants to hurt you. In those situations, fight like hell.

Do as They Say

Imagine you are working alone in your boutique, a convenience store or fast food restaurant. A guy comes in, points a gun, and says, "This is a robbery. Give me the money." Be calm. Look him in the eye and tell him the money is in the register. Ask him: "Do you want me to open the register, or do you want to open it?" Asking questions shows him that you understand he is in charge and that you will comply. Ask what he wants you to put the money in. Don't move without asking him if you can. Most robbers get high on alcohol and/or drugs before they pull the job. They are cognitively impaired. If you make startling movements, you will frighten them and they will shoot. Try to be as calm as possible, and don't let the Disbelief, Disorientation and Overwhelming Fear prevail.

The goal in these types of "stickup" situations is to project the image of a person who can face adversity and will get through it. You neither want to be a braggart nor show extreme cowardice. Simply let the robber have the money and get away.

Chapter 14

Surviving with Dignity

As I have stated throughout this book, I am a big believer in fighting and resistance. I recognize, however, that not everyone is like me. If you read this entire book and/or attended one of my presentations, but you still say to yourself, "I can't. I cannot do this." That's okay.

You need to know that Disbelief, Disorientation and Overwhelming Fear can be overcome. It takes practice in non-threatening situations and wanting to never be a victim. It takes risking being a new person, a person who will become in charge of her circumstances. According to the Rape, Abuse and Incest National Network (RAINN), every two and a half minutes, somewhere in America, someone is being sexually assaulted. One in six American women are victims of sexual assault and one in 33 men. In 2004-2005 there was an average annual 200,780 victims of rape, attempted rape or sexual assault. About 44% of rape victims are under age 18 and 80% are under age 30.

Although this number has fallen by more than 69%, it is still too high. I share this number with you not to frighten you, but to impress upon you that rape happens. Rape happens to women throughout the country – strong, bright women who were unable to stop it. If there is any blessing in this large number of rape victims, it is that we, as a society, are forced to become more aware of the problem.

We know that the victim is not the culprit. She does not provoke the rape, nor is she at fault for failing to stop it. For some of you, that may seem like an obvious statement, but it always amazes me how many victims, for one reason or another, feel like they did something wrong – that they did something that was improper and they caused the rapist to attack. That's just not the case. If you are the victim of rape, you need to know that you have done nothing wrong. You are not the bad person. You are the good person. Due to the shame that accompanies rape, according to RAINN, an estimated 41% of rapes are not reported.

If you are the victim of rape, you need to know that help is available. A friend of mine, Dr. Jo Ann Brannock, is a clinical psychologist in Fullerton. She says it is important for a rape victim to believe that "healing is possible." Victims of any violent crime, but especially one as traumatic as rape, often suffer from post-traumatic stress disorder (PTSD). They suffer the same types of nightmares, flashbacks and difficulty sleeping as combat soldiers. Unfortunately, PTSD often accompanies depression and other problems of physical and mental health, as well as self-destructive behavior such as alcohol and drug abuse and self-mutilation through cutting or burning. Emotional symptoms of rape can persist for years after the incident and it's never too late to seek help.

Rape victims need to work with a therapist to identify coping mechanisms, and they need to establish a strong support network of friends and family. As much as someone may want to recede from the world to hide in shame, it is very important for a rape victim to stay connected to loved ones. I often tell the husbands and boyfriends of a rape victim that their job in this difficult time is to provide unconditional love, understanding and support. They need to recognize that a woman who has been assaulted feels violated and unsafe, and that sexual intimacy is the furthest thing from her mind. The man needs to give her time to heal by providing support and verbal encouragement.

At the beginning of this book, I told you the story of the police officer's wife who had been brutally raped and beaten. The image of her helpless, broken body lying on the hospital gurney will never leave me. I know that she suffered immeasurable pain during the attack, and I know that she had a lifetime of healing ahead of her. But I agree with Dr. Brannock that healing is possible. If you, like the officer's wife, are made to suffer something so horrible as a sexual assault, your whole purpose will be to survive with dignity. Survive with dignity in everything you do. The medical doctors can fix your bruises and broken bones, but don't neglect to heal your heart and mind too. It will take a lot of work, but it really is possible. I promise.

She Bear

Chapter 15

A Survivor of an Attempted Abduction

Sam is a neighbor of our daughter-in-law. Approximately two years ago Janel, our daughter-in-law, asked me to contact Sam and debrief her on her experience of attempted abduction. This is Sam's story.

Sam was 30-years-old at the time of the abduction. Sam was married to Dave, a handsome 30-something year old. They were recent proud parents of a baby girl. Sam and Dave were successfully living in Costa Mesa, California, in an affluent neighborhood. The neighborhood was very cohesive, with block parties on the 4th of July and neighborhood birthday parties for the many children that were being raised there. Thus, Sam knew several male neighbors. (None of whom were the suspects in this case study).

It was a beautiful, sunny California November day in 2003. Sam and Dave live close to Newport Beach, California.

Their community is very close to the ocean. One day Dave was at work and Sam was at home. She was feeling ill and decided to make a pot of soup. Sam entered her two-door Saab convertible (the top was up) and drove to the market to buy the ingredients to make soup. She had worked 13 days in a row and was tired and feeling poorly from lack of rest.

Sam went through the drive-thru of a fast food restaurant and bought a hamburger. She then proceeded to the supermarket. The market was on a major street and was well attended. Parking was available to the front of the market and on the east side of the supermarket. Sam released her seatbelt as she pulled into a parking spot on the side of the market (first row up against the building) in a marked stall. There were several other cars in the area as well as people moving about in the very large parking lot.

The sun was warm in the car. Sam started feeling better and unwrapped her hamburger. She managed one bite when she heard the passenger car door open.

"My mind immediately thought it must be a neighbor or someone I know… then I heard a man's voice (one that I had never heard before) say in an almost sweet innocent way " Excuse me Ma'am?" Even though the voice sounded harmless, I knew in that moment how wrong and how brazen it was that a stranger would open my passenger side door (whether he had a question or needed directions, etc., which was what it sounded like it could have been with the "Excuse me Ma'am question)," Sam said.

"It caught me so off guard that my mind sped up. It was working faster and faster to try and reason the situation at hand. Then the unbelievable happened; the stranger was getting into my car with me. It was happening so fast yet it seemed to be in slow motion because my mind was racing. As he was leaning in to sit in the seat I immediately knew this was a bad situation. I knew in my gut that nothing good could come out of this.

"What I didn't know yet was why was he getting into my car and what he wanted. I was in a state of such confusion, trying desperately to make some sense of something so completely unexpected. Before he was fully seated I started hitting him and trying to push him back out of the car. I just kept swinging and cursing at him. I was yelling, 'What are you doing! Get out!' But he was getting in, no matter what I did. I was never so angry in all my life. I felt like a mad dog… how dare him! And then all of a sudden in my fury, I heard the passenger side door shut. It sounded so final, like all my fighting and yelling was doing nothing to stop whatever was about to happen. Now we were shoulder to shoulder in my very small car.

"I was in such utter disbelief that things became more exaggerated in slow motion. Still swinging at him I caught a glimpse of a silver object moving up the right side of my body. As I looked down it was pointed at the right side of my neck.

"The stranger pushed a Smith and Wesson 40 caliber auto loading pistol against the side of my neck. I heard a silent voice in my gut: 'This cannot be happening!' My anger immediately turned to fear – fear like I have never known. Fear I never want to know again. I heard my own guttural voice (which I hardly recognized as my own) scream 'No!' and immediately started to fumble with my left hand to find the door handle. Then he spoke, with an angry tone and his teeth clenched he said 'don't panic!'

"I couldn't believe this was the same person who said 'Excuse me, Ma'am.' The sound of his voice now would never be forgotten. I felt like I had made him really angry because I was fighting and not complying. Did I make this even worse for myself? I knew something horrible was going to happen and just when I started feeling that this was going to be "it" I heard that voice deep down in my gut. It sounded like it was me, but about three octaves lower. A voice that was not to be reckoned with. And it said slowly and with more power than that Smith and Wesson: This is NOT going to happen to me!

"If I could just make it out of this car, I thought, then at least I can be shot in the parking lot and I will never have to go with him – he will never be able to touch me. He will not decide where and when I die or what I have to endure before that time. There are things worse than death and now the potential of dying in the parking lot of the local grocery store was hands down the better alternative – one that I could choose for myself. I struggled to fight him with my right arm while my left was fumbling desperately to release the door handle. But it was like I had no coordination now. The fear and probably overload of adrenaline made my legs feel heavy and numb as if they were paralyzed and my arms were jerky and hard to control.

"I felt and fought like a wild animal that was caught and trapped like prey. Then with an accidental open handed hit to his left ear, through our flailing arms, I caught a glimpse of him shaking his head and holding his arms up the way a boxer protects his face. I knew that was it… my moment. My opportunity. At the same time my fumbling left hand had managed to release the door handle. I exited the vehicle still screaming 'No.' I tried to run toward the major intersection – ankles seeming to give way and I fell at least two times. Now I was certain I would be shot.

"I thought my assailant must be right behind me. Two men ran to me. In my confused state I thought they might too be a danger. I fell again, got up and again tried to run. I started to realize that he couldn't be behind me at this point. Now I looked back hoping to see my car driving out of the parking lot. I wanted so badly to believe that this guy wanted my car but knew from the moment he got in the car with me that that was not the case.

"As I looked, my car was still sitting in the parking space, still running with both doors wide open and I caught a glimpse of the assailant climbing over an eight foot wall that enclosed that section of the parking lot. Fixated on this guy getting away, I could see out of the corner of my eyes that there were a few people getting closer to me. Now a 50-something year old female reached me. I knew the woman was safe. This 50-something year old darling (I never learned her name nor have I seen her again) held me and softly told me I was safe. The woman rocked me back and forth. I have never forgotten that kindness and have thought that perhaps it was an angel.

"Several people had called 911 and the police arrived quickly. The woman disappeared. These are the facts of what happened at the scene, but is certainly not the end of my story," Sam said.

Sam's assailant climbed the wall, which terminated at the roof of a carport of an adjacent apartment building. The assailant jumped from the roof to the driveway below. Two men were in the carport assembling their fishing gear. To their surprise the assailant jumped and landed in front of them. He dropped his pistol. The pistol skidded almost to the foot of one of the two men. The suspect retrieved the pistol and ran. The two men were aware of Sam's screams and went to the market parking lot. The suspect was now the subject of a police search. A perimeter was established. Helicopters, squad cars and detective units searched. The suspect was located hiding in a dumpster.

The police attempted to talk the suspect into surrender. Instead, the suspect used the discarded plastic garbage bags in the dumpster to suffocate himself to death, and the police found the gun just outside the dumpster.

The police held Sam in the parking lot for approximately four hours. Several different officers asked her questions. Sam felt so alone. Dave, her husband, could not be contacted. Ironically, Dave's boss was in the area and heard the commotion. He arrived on at scene. His presence comforted Sam.

Dave arrived much later. He approached an officer and told the officer he had to see the person that did this to his wife. He was denied. The head detective told Dave that the suspect was deceased.

Now thoughts played in Sam's conscious. She remembered the guttural screams she made. Those screams haunted Sam for several weeks. She remembered the terrible cursing words she used. She remembered the car door closing and how trapped she felt. The primal voice she heard deep in her gut saying "No, this is not going to happen to me – I am not going to be assaulted." One of the strikes Sam had delivered to her assailant was an open hand over his ear, which is very effective. This caused the suspect to shake his head. At the same time Sam found the door handle and opened the door and escaped. The open hand over the ear was probably what allowed that escape.

As Sam ran, it was as though she had lost control of her limbs. She especially remembers her ankles giving way. Sam thought she would certainly be shot, but she did not fear being shot nor death as much as she feared being raped. She remembers thinking being shot is the better alternative. She found some kind of peace in that horrible alternative.

Sam had looked back, expecting the suspect to be behind her. She hoped she would see the suspect in her car driving away. Sam told me she would have given him her car, money or any possession. Those were not important. The police, however, mistakenly thought Sam had fought this hard to protect her car.

For more than three weeks Sam continued to hear the suspect's voice. She could still see his tense, clenched mouth and jaw and she continued to feel the suspect's coarse, unwashed hair on her hands. Women that have as traumatic an experience as Sam, usually remember something about the feel of their assailant. Oftentimes it is the suspect's bad breath against her face or the feel of his skin.

Sam is a beautiful, brilliant woman. The police underestimated her power of observation. The detectives thought this woman, who has never been around weapons, could not possibly identify the pistol. Sam was shown several pictures of various pistols. She successfully pointed out the Smith and Wesson. She even told them of the pistols mat finish.

During one of her interviews, a superior officer (assumed by Sam) entered the interview room and told Sam she was very lucky and to never fight like that again. She could have been killed trying to save her car. SAVE HER CAR! Sam wanted to scream, "I did not give a damn about the car." She did not do so. When the superior left the room, the case detective quietly told Sam "you did the right thing." Well done detective.

The aftermath of the event was one of both pain and support. Sam was surrounded by well wishing people following her harrowing experience. Shortly thereafter she was alone. I interpret the feeling Sam described as similar to someone that has lost a loved one. Following the death, the person is surrounded by love and well-wishers. Almost immediately after the conclusion of the funeral, the person is alone. Sam had a similar lonely feeling. The local newspaper printed articles about the plight of the now dead perpetrator. The columnist portrayed the suspect as a misguided veteran that was trying to steal a car. Once again Sam thought no one understood. People close to Sam including Dave, her husband, thought Sam should "get over it" and move on. She was still injured and not ready to move on.

Sam would sit and stare out the window. She was frightened to open the door for any male person. She was haunted by the memory of her own guttural screams. She heard them over and over again. For over three weeks Sam felt the suspect's coarse hair between her fingers.

Dave, her husband, wanted her to "move on and get over it." Sam began to resent Dave and closed him and others out. She thought that no one understood. It deteriorated to the point that Sam no longer cared if her marriage would end.

Fortunately, Sam and Dave had dinner with an old friend of mine, Susan Saxe Clifford. Susan is a police psychologist that I have known since she was a new psychologist working for the Los Angeles Police Department. That was a long time ago. Susan now has a very successful private practice. The Fullerton Police Department oftentimes uses Susan for pre-screening of applicants or for trauma counseling for police officers. The meeting between Sam and Susan was by chance. Sam was unaware of Susan's occupation or expertise. During the dinner conversation Sam revealed her anguish to Susan.

Susan recognized that Sam was in trouble. Susan told Sam she should see a trauma counselor as quickly as possible. Sam fortunately took Susan's advice. She engaged in counseling and has recovered as much as is possible after going though such a traumatic event. It is important that women seek counseling after an attack, whether it happened a month ago or ten years ago. The emotional damage of a rape or attempted attack can be the worst part of the entire situation.

Today Sam is an advocate for women's safety. She will see a lone female seated in a car with unlocked doors. Sam will approach, knock on the window and ask the female to do her a favor and lock her doors. Sam asked me to relate this to the readers of this book. "Fight, chief – you tell people to fight." I promised her I would.

Chapter 16

A Survivor of an Attempted Kidnapping

Claris and her new boyfriend were night clubbing. They visited several bars and were both intoxicated. At around 1 a.m. the couple returned to their care that was parked in a parking lot behind several businesses. Her boyfriend was getting ill. He vomited, entered the car and passed out.

Claris sat in the car and dozed off. She awakened and was cold. She was about to start the car for warmth when there was a knock on her window. Claris rolled down the window. A male stood outside. He told Claris her companion had been drinking. She remembers the following confrontation:

Claris: Yeah, what is it to you?

Man: I'm a cop. I need to see your ID.

Claris: What? (She started looking for her driver's license in her purse.)

Man: I need you to step out of the car. (Claris complied.)

Man: Face the car and give me your ID.

An argument ensued in which the male told Claris she was about to drive intoxicated. Claris disagreed. The argument continued and Claris said, "Okay just give me a ticket or whatever."

Man: You need to go to my car so I can run your license (the male now possessed Claris' driver's license.)

The man pretended to be talking on an invisible radio. Claris told him, "I need to wake-up my boyfriend and let him know." The man said no and grabbed Claris as she started to walk toward her vehicle. He put Claris in a headlock and said, "You're resisting arrest." Claris started shouting for her boyfriend. The man dragged Claris to his van and opened the sliding door. Claris fought and continued to call for her boyfriend. Claris told him, "You ain't no cop." He argued he was. Claris finally shouted, "Let me see your badge."

The man forced Claris into the van and pushed her down between the front seats. He told Claris he was taking her to book her. Claris knew her dire circumstance. She told the suspect she was menstruating. The suspect told her he wasn't going to do anything. Claris said she was pregnant and asked to be allowed to return to her boyfriend.

She told the man that if he would let her go she wouldn't say anything.

The man started the van and drove off with Claris pinned between the seats and crying. He pretended to talk on an imaginary radio. After about 15 minutes of driving, with Claris crying and pleading, Claris told the suspect she was getting sick. The suspect told her to go ahead, and Claris vomited.

Claris' hand felt a heavy object on the passenger seat. She confiscated it and put it up her sleeve, hoping to use it as a weapon and escape.

Claris was now aware that the van was not on a road and was going down a hill. The van stopped. The man told her to get up. Claris asked, "What do you want?" He said, "This is where I'm going to rape you." He told Claris to take off her clothes. Claris fought as the suspect dragged her out of the van and started disrobing her. The suspect stripped her naked and started kissing her. Claris attempted to push him away and kept repeating, "Leave me alone."

The van was stuck. The man took Claris back to the van. She continued pleading with him to let her go and she would not "say anything." Claris told him she would help him with the van. He then threw Claris her shirt and told her to put it on. As she was attempting to put her shirt on (while being seated in the van), she observed a car approaching. Claris started honking the horn. The man pushed her back and told her to "shut up" as she kicked at him and screamed for help. The approaching car stopped. Claris mustered all her strength and pushed the suspect off her. She ran from the van, now completely naked. She ran to the stopped vehicle and said, "Help, he's trying to rape me."

Claris looked in the vehicle and observed a man and woman. The woman looked "awkward." Claris thought "Oh no, he is trying to do the same thing to her."

Claris found herself in a canyon. She started to run. She ran into the brush and continued to run. She then hid in the bushes. She heard voices and thought people were after her. She moved with stealth, trying not to make any noise. Claris heard the suspect attempting to release the van and heard other voices. Claris continued to move away into the hills. She saw people walking with flashlights and thought the attacker was looking for her. She hid in the bushes. Continuing her quiet movement, she fell several times. The sun started coming up. She saw vehicle headlights and went toward them. She came to benches and a shed. Still thinking the suspect was pursuing her, Claris picked up an empty bottle for defense and continued walking. Coming upon a cabin, she suspected danger. She continued walking and came to a road. She did not stop, frightened the suspect would be in one of the cars. Claris continued to walk until she came upon another road. Now naked, hurt and exhausted, she sat down. She heard men talking and saw two cars.

Claris realized she was too exhausted to continue to flee. She decided to take a chance. She walked up to one of the men and said, "I need help." The man just looked at her. He then walked toward her. Claris thought "Oh, no." The man took off his jacket and covered Claris. Claris collapsed. The two men covered her with a blanket. One called for help on his cell telephone. A sheriff's deputy arrived. Claris, in her confused state, asked the deputy if he was going to rape her. The deputy said, "No, I am here to help you."

Other police cars arrived and Claris finally realized she was now safe. The authorities located the stuck van. In the van was

Claris' clothing and identification. The suspect was located and arrested.

Because Claris was drunk, it impaired her from using her Inner Sense of Danger and stopped her from not asking for the police officer's identification. She knew the male was not acting appropriately as a police officer should, but in her inebriated state she was unable to think as clearly as she might have. She also had a drunk, useless boyfriend in the car. Your man should be your defender. My wife often says your man should be willing to slay dragons for you. Choose a man who will.

Next, Claris suffered from Disbelief, Disorientation and Overwhelming Fear. Her panicked state caused her to lose reason. Not until she was exhausted did she seek assistance and even then was suspicious of the deputy.

This is a natural response to such a dangerous situation. Claris did nothing wrong, but her story is a testament to other women on how to overcome fear and trust their instincts. That being said, Claris was a warrior. She fought, struggled and fled naked into the night. She was in a cold canyon all night thinking any number of people were pursuing her. She continued on with a warrior's mentality.

Trust your Inner Sense of Danger. Remember escape and evasion is most easily accomplished at the original point of your capture.

She Bear

Chapter 17

Never Quit Fighting

One of my favorite poets is Robert W. Service. He grew up in Scotland and immigrated to Canada at the age of 22. After traveling throughout British Columbia and the Western United States, Service settled in the Yukon and began to write poetry. I am a big fan of Service's work, which usually talks about the Yukon and the cold and survival through tough times. One of his poems in the book, Rhymes of a Rolling Stone, is about a guy who is lost.

The Quitter, by Robert Service
When you're lost in the wild, and you're scared as a child,
And Death looks you bang in the eye,
And you're sore as a boil, it's according to Hoyle
To cock your revolver and…die.
But the Code of a Man says: "Fight all you can,"
And self-dissolution is barred.
In hunger and woe, oh, it's easy to blow…
It's the hell-served-for-breakfast that's hard.

"You're sick of the game!" Well, now, that's a shame.
You're young and you're brave and you're bright.
"You've had a raw deal!" I know – but don't squeal,
Buck up, do your damnedest, and fight.
It's the plugging away that will win you the day,
So don't be a piker, old pard!
Just draw on your grit; it's so easy to quit:
It's the keeping-your-chin-up that's hard.
It's easy to cry that you're beaten – and die;
It's easy to crawfish and crawl;
But to fight and to fight when hope's out of sight –
Why, that's the best game of them all!
And though you come out of each grueling bout,
All broken and beaten and scarred,
Just have one more try – it's dead easy to die,
It's the keeping-on-living that's hard.

If you ever find yourself in a tough situation that seems impossible to conquer, I hope you will remember some of the lines in this poem, and I hope you will remember the things we have talked about in this book. First, remember you must always be aware of your environment. If you are, you will know when you are walking into a potentially perilous situation. Second, listen to your Inner Sense of Danger, and be on the lookout for avenues of escape. Third, don't be afraid to use your intellect, strength and determination to dominate the situation. And if all else fails, let loose with the head butt or any attack to the groin to shock and disarm your attacker. He will momentarily release you. Use this window of opportunity to make your escape.

Above all, remember that you are smarter than your attacker. Like the She Bear, be fierce and you will overcome any dangerous situation and walk away with an inner strength more powerful than any physical force.

She Bear

QUICK SUMMARY

Instinctually Behavior in an Attack
1. Disbelief: Believing that this cannot be happening to me and mistakenly thinking that everything will be okay.
2. Disorientation: A feeling of floating over one's own body and feeling frozen during the attack.
3. Overwhelming Fear: A fear so deep that the victim shakes and cries–a fear so powerful that it renders the victim helpless and pliable.

Overcoming Instinctually Behavior
1. Listen to your Inner Sense of Danger: Use your God-given ability to assess a situation that doesn't feel right.
2. Change your mindset: The criminals who attack women are dumb and skittish and the slightest bit of resistance (cuss, yell, use pepper spray) will send him away.
3. Smarts over strength: Realize that using the techniques included in this book will show you that your intellect will overcome the type of criminal that attacks women.

Simple Safety in Public and at Home
1. Scan a room before entering.
2. Buy pepper spray.
3. Lock doors and windows.
4. Don't open doors for strangers.
5. Get a dog.
6. Purchase an alarm.
7. Create a safe room.

Car Safety
1. Lock the doors.
2. Roll up windows.
3. Carry a cell phone.
4. Stop 1½ car lengths behind the limit line at an intersection.
5. Being followed? Make three right turns.
6. Cause a crash if necessary.
7. Find a well-lit place to exchange accident information.
8. Jump out of the car if necessary.

Date Rape
1. Tell the person you don't want to go any further.
2. If sex is forced, bite him on the cheek as hard as you can.
3. Seek counseling.
4. Remember that the rape is not your fault.

Surviving a Rape
1. Head butt the criminal.
2. Grab his testacies.
3. If raped, go straight to the hospital.
4. Make a report to the police.
5. Seek counseling.
6. Remember that the attack is never your fault.

INDEX

Abduction, 79
Abuse, 9, 75, 76
Accident, 56, 58, 100
Action(s), 12, 14, 40, 61, 71
Active techniques, 43
adrenaline, 82
Advice, 64, 70, 87
Advocate, 64, 87
Alarm, 52, 99
Alarm system, 52
Alcohol, 11, 74, 76
Alert, 22, 32, 37, 44, 69
Alert police, 69
Alone, 11, 14, 21, 22, 31, 32, 34, 37, 40, 45, 51, 52, 56-58, 73, 84, 86, 91
Ambushes, 57
Ammunition, 35, 67
Anger, 64, 81
Anguish, 87
Approach(ed), 8, 26, 39, 51, 55, 59, 84, 87
Armed gunmen, 72
Arsenal, 9
Assailant, 83
Assault, 9, 11, 18, 25, 65, 75, 77
Assistance, 4, 93
Attack, 19, 76, 77, 87, 96, 99, 100
Attacker(s), 26, 38, 45, 47, 58, 59
Attitude, 32, 33
Authorities, 69, 73, 93
Awareness, 50
Bandit(s), 13, 27, 28
Bank robberies, 28
Bank robbers, 27, 28
Behavior, 19, 21, 28, 38, 69, 76, 99
Being
   alert, 22
   confident, 71
   followed, 57, 100
   victims, 34
Broken bones, 60, 77
Brute strength, 47
Burglar(s), 50, 51, 52
California law, 68
Call boxes, 56
Capable women, 8

Capital punishment, 12
Captive, 73
Captors, 73
Capture, 93
Car
   approaching, 91
   description, 59
   door(s), 55, 56, 61, 80, 84
   length, 57, 100
   safety, 55, 57, 100
Carjackers, 58
Carport, 27, 83, 84
Carry keys, 45
Carry-on luggage, 46
Cash, 50
Cell phones, 53
Challenge, 21
Chances, 51, 59, 60
Children, 40, 46, 55, 79
Clinical psychologist, 76
Comforting, 84
Command, 26
Commanding officer(s), 27, 31, 67, 69
Commotion, 58, 72, 84
Companion, 51, 89
Company, 50, 51, 59
Confusion, 72, 81
Connection, 53, 73
Conscious mind, 40
Consequence, 38
Contact, 45, 69, 79
Control, 26, 27, 38, 45, 64, 68, 69, 82, 85
Conversation, 38, 87, 89
Coping mechanisms, 77
Counseling, 87, 100
Course, 18, 27, 52, 58, 71
Crash, 58, 59, 71, 100
Crash-course, 58
Crime, 26, 63, 28, 69, 76
Criminal
   mind, 28
   will, 56
   world, 50
Crook, 33, 34
Culprit, 76

Cursing, 81, 84
Dangerous situation(s), 22, 43, 93, 97
Date Rape, 63, 64, 100
Deadbolt, 52
Dealer(s), 60, 61
Defender, 93
Defense, 92
Defenseless, 31
Depression, 76
Detective units, 84
Detective's instruction, 70
Dignity, 5, 75, 77
Direction(s), 40, 55, 72, 80
Discipline, 26
Disconnectedness, 18
Disconnection, 64
Disorder, 76
Disorientation, 8, 9, 15, 17, 23, 32, 33, 74, 75, 93
Domestic violence, 65
Dominance, 19, 33, 34
Drive, 11, 50, 56-60, 90
Driver's
   license, 89, 90
   seat, 34
Driveway, 83
Driving, 34, 38, 40, 57, 83, 85, 91
Drop, 60, 61
Duck, 40
Elevator(s), 37, 38
Emails, 68
Emotion, 19
Encouragement, 4, 77
Enforcement, 8, 26, 28, 35, 69
Evasion, 93
Evidence, 64, 65
Exit plan, 44
Experience Disbelief, 8
Expression(s), 3, 32, 43
Extensive training, 22
Family(ies), 49, 50, 69, 77
Fastest reaction, 61
Fatal shooting, 27
Fatalities, 17
FBI, 26
Felons, 46
Female, 2, 8, 9, 22, 27, 34, 51, 68, 83, 87
Fire, 27, 50
Firearm, 44
Flashbacks, 76

Flashlights, 92
Follow, 5, 38, 39, 59
Following, 4, 12, 18, 32, 57, 58, 68, 86, 89
Friend, 3, 7, 40, 56, 60, 76, 87
Future prosecution, 69
Garage, 38, 56
Gas
   pedal, 61
   station, 11, 13, 14, 38, 39
   tanks, 39
Getaway car, 27
Gift, 21, 22
Giving advice, 4
Goal, 23, 47, 64, 74
Grab, 19, 31, 44, 47, 48, 56, 61, 100
Grizzly bear, 7-9
Gun owner, 44
Gunmen, 71, 72, 73
Guns, 12, 26, 27, 44
Gut, 81, 82, 84
Hair(s), 14, 32, 85, 86
Head, 12, 28, 32, 35, 38, 46, 47, 49, 60, 61, 82, 84, 85, 96, 100
Helpless(ness), 19, 47, 77, 99
Hit, 46, 65, 82
Holding, 5, 26, 27, 44, 82
Home
   insurance, 52
   safety, 5, 49
Hope, 5, 60, 96
Hostage crisis, 5, 71
Hostage situations, 71
Hour(s), 27, 37, 59, 60, 64, 80, 84
Identification, 93
Illegal weapons, 25
Information, 46, 58, 59, 100
Injury(ies), 3, 25, 68
Inner
   power, 21
   voice, 22
Inner Sense of Danger, 5, 9, 18, 21-23, 32, 34, 35, 37-41, 43, 51, 81, 93, 96, 99
Instinctually behavior, 99
Instructions, 45
Instructor, 61
Insurance
   company, 59
   purposes, 58
Intellect, 32, 35, 96, 99
Intersection, 57, 58, 83, 100

Index

Interview(s), 12, 86
Intimidators, 33, 35
Intruders, 50
Intuition, 21
Jaw, 8, 85
Jogging, 34, 40
Jump out, 7, 59-61, 100
Jump-and-roll maneuver, 60
Key(s), 45, 46, 55
Kidnapper, 59, 61
Killer(s), 12
Kindness, 83
Knife, 47, 58
Knowledge, 4, 28
LAPD's SWAT, 35
Law enforcement, 8, 26, 28, 35, 69
Lead(s), 27, 32, 63
Learned behavior, 19, 21
License, 32, 58, 59, 89, 90
Limit line, 57, 59, 100
Live, 7, 55, 79
Lock, 50, 52, 55, 56, 59, 87, 99, 100
Love, 67, 77, 86
Male
   person, 86
   robber, 27
Malice, 14
Mall, 38, 45, 71
Manner, 11, 39
Market, 80, 84
Martial arts, 46
Mask(s), 27, 28, 44
Maximum effect, 46
Medical doctors, 77
Mental health, 76
Message, 3, 32, 33, 69
Military tactics, 25
Minor fender-bender, 58
Movement(s), 72, 92, 74
Near-death experience, 18
Neck, 14, 47, 81
Neighbor, 40, 79, 80
Neighborhood(s), 26, 49, 60, 79
New
   door, 52
   life, 13
   mindset, 27
   person, 75
   psychologist, 87
Night Stalker, 49

Nose, 45-47
Obscene gestures, 57
Office, 28, 37, 51, 68, 71
Officer's, 60, 64, 77, 93
Open, 5, 18, 40, 49-51, 56, 59, 61, 73, 80, 82, 83, 85, 86, 99
Opportunity, 57, 82, 96
Organization, 17, 26
Outcome, 27, 71
Overcoming
   disbelief, 23
   fear, 11
Overwhelming fear, 8, 9, 15, 17-19, 23, 32, 33, 74, 75, 93, 99
Pain, 47, 48, 60, 65, 77, 86
Panicked state, 93
Paralysis, 8, 14, 18
Parking, 38, 45, 56, 80, 82-84, 89
Passenger(s), 46, 55, 60, 71, 80, 81, 91
Passenger('s) seat, 60, 91
Pay phone, 56
Pepper spray, 44-47
Perceptions, 9
Permit, 44, 46
Perpetrator(s), 68, 86
Personal connection, 73
Pets, 68
Phone, 50, 52, 53, 56, 59, 68, 69, 100
Physical examination, 65
Physical strength, 29
Picture, 21, 37
Police
   officers, 13, 14, 25, 27, 69, 87
   psychologist, 87
   situation, 25
   station, 58, 59
Possession, 85
Post-traumatic, 76
Potential dangers, 22
Potential victim, 2
Power, 5, 21, 82, 85
Practice, 35, 41, 51, 55, 57, 75, 87
Predators, 8
Preventative actions, 40
Prey, 8, 82
Privacy, 52
Proactive, 55
Problem(s), 21, 57, 67, 76
Property, 33, 68

Protection, 1, 44, 52
Protective fighter, 2
Protocol, 37, 38
Public, 22, 49, 56, 99
   eye, 22
   places, 56
Purchase, 45, 46, 52, 99
Raid, 25
RAINN, 75, 76
Rape victim(s), 17, 18, 32, 75-77
Rapist(s), 19, 31, 34, 73, 76
Reaction, 13, 19, 22, 61, 65, 72
Reaction time, 61
Remorse, 12
Repeating, 50, 91
Report(s), 3, 17, 18, 64, 68, 69, 100
Reprisals, 68
Residence, 26
Response, 13, 61, 72, 93
Return(ing), 27, 38, 90
Revolver, 26, 95
Richard Ramirez, 49-50
Risk(ing), 37, 38, 40, 72, 75
Robber(s), 27-29, 34, 74
Robbery, 17, 28, 43, 44, 71-73
Run, 12, 46, 56, 72, 83, 90, 92
Running car, 34
Safe room, 52, 99
Safety, 43, 55, 99
Saying No, 64, 65, 84
Scam(s), 38, 40
School, 47, 55, 61, 71
Counseling, 87, 100
Self-defense, 45, 46
Self-dissolution, 95
Self-mutilation, 76
Sense of Danger, 5, 9, 18, 21-23, 32, 34, 35, 37-41, 43, 51, 81, 93, 96, 99
Service, 1, 22, 52, 95
Sexual assault, 65, 75, 77
Sexual intercourse, 64
Sexual intimacy, 77
Shame, 64, 76, 77, 95
Shock, 19, 33, 47, 64, 96
Shooting, 12, 26, 27, 72, 74
Shopping, 45, 55, 71
Shoulder, 57, 81
Shower, 31, 64
Sign, 57, 59, 65
Signals, 22, 63
Silent voice, 81

Situations, 1, 5, 9, 22, 37, 43, 60, 68, 71, 73-75
Skillful predator, 8
SLA, 26, 27
Smarter, 21, 29, 96
Society, 9, 32, 76
Sociopath, 12
Soldiers, 76
Solution, 57
Special Investigations, 27, 28
Special training, 46
Special Weapons, 1, 25
Spray, 44-47, 99
Stalkers, 68, 69
Stalking(s) 66, 68-69
Standard behavior, 38
Standing, 31, 37, 68, 71
Steal, 60, 86
Stealth, 92
Steering wheel, 61
Stereotype, 32
Stickup, 12, 34, 74
Stop sign, 57, 59
Stopped vehicle, 91
Store security, 26
Stores, 38, 44, 46
Stranger(s), 38, 50, 68, 80, 81, 99
Street, 9, 26, 32, 34, 40, 45, 60, 80
Strength, 4, 5, 29, 31, 47, 91, 96, 97, 99
Stress, 28, 76
Strong
   emotions, 5
   people, 9
   sixth, 21
Submissiveness, 32
Survival, 13, 95
Suspect(s), 28, 85
SWAT, 27, 67
Swinging, 81
Tactical awareness, 2
Tactics, 1, 5, 25, 60, 73
Tactics unit, 1, 25
Technique(s), 38, 43, 46, 47, 57, 99
Testicle-grabbing techniques, 38
Therapist, 77
Throat, 8, 45, 49
Tools, 8, 9, 22
Trauma, 64, 87
Traumatic
   event, 87
   experience, 85

Index

Trigger, 44, 61
Trust, 9, 40, 93
Truth, 4, 55, 64
Turn, 9, 22, 45, 52, 59
Unacceptable behavior, 69
Unconditional love, 77
Undercover officer, 60
Unlocked door, 56
Unsafe, 56, 77
Ursus horribilis, 8
Valor, 71
Value, 21, 69
Vehicle(s), 55, 58, 83
Victim
    advocate, 64
    helpless, 19, 99
Victimization, 13, 32
Violent crime, 76
Violent death, 14
Voice(s), 22, 35, 38, 39, 80-82, 84, 85, 92
Walter Kelbach, 11
Warrior's mentality, 93
Watch, 26, 33, 34, 38, 46, 59
Weapon(s), 25, 31, 44, 46, 72, 85, 91
Well-lit, 38, 58, 59, 100
Woman's reaction, 65
Women's safety, 5, 87
Working, 1, 3, 11, 26, 28, 73, 80, 87